HARLEQUINADE

A Farce in One Act

by Terence Rattigan

samuelfrench.co.uk

Copyright © 1949 by Samuel French Ltd
All Rights Reserved

HARLEQUINADE is fully protected under the copyright laws of the British Commonwealth, including Canada, the United States of America, and all other countries of the Copyright Union. All rights, including professional and amateur stage productions, recitation, lecturing, public reading, motion picture, radio broadcasting, television and the rights of translation into foreign languages are strictly reserved.

ISBN 978-0-573-02094-0

www.samuelfrench.co.uk
www.samuelfrench.com

For Amateur Production Enquiries

United Kingdom and World
excluding North America

plays@samuelfrench.co.uk

020 7255 4302/01

Each title is subject to availability from Samuel French, depending upon country of performance.

CAUTION: Professional and amateur producers are hereby warned that *HARLEQUINADE* is subject to a licensing fee. Publication of this play does not imply availability for performance. Both amateurs and professionals considering a production are strongly advised to apply to the appropriate agent before starting rehearsals, advertising, or booking a theatre. A licensing fee must be paid whether the title is presented for charity or gain and whether or not admission is charged.

The professional rights in this play are controlled by Alan Brodie Representation Ltd, Paddock Suite, The Courtyard, 55 Charterhouse Street, London EC1M 6HA www.alanbrodie.com.

No one shall make any changes in this title for the purpose of production. No part of this book may be reproduced, stored in a retrieval system, or transmitted in any form, by any means, now known or yet to be invented, including mechanical, electronic, photocopying, recording, videotaping, or otherwise, without the prior written permission of the publisher. No one shall upload this title, or part of this title, to any social media websites.

The right of Terence Rattigan to be identified as author of this work has been asserted in accordance with Section 77 of the Copyright, Designs and Patents Act 1988.

THINKING ABOUT PERFORMING A SHOW?

There are thousands of plays and musicals available to perform from Samuel French right now, and applying for a licence is easier and more affordable than you might think

---

From classic plays to brand new musicals, from monologues to epic dramas, there are shows for everyone.

Plays and musicals are protected by copyright law, so if you want to perform them, the first thing you'll need is a licence. This simple process helps support the playwright by ensuring they get paid for their work and means that you'll have the documents you need to stage the show in public.

Not all our shows are available to perform all the time, so it's important to check and apply for a licence before you start rehearsals or commit to doing the show.

LEARN MORE & FIND THOUSANDS OF SHOWS

Browse our full range of plays and musicals, and find out more about how to license a show

www.samuelfrench.co.uk/perform

Talk to the friendly experts in our Licensing team for advice on choosing a show and help with licensing

plays@samuelfrench.co.uk   020 7387 9373

Acting Editions
BORN TO PERFORM

Playscripts designed from the ground up to work the way you do in rehearsal, performance and study

Larger, clearer text for easier reading

Wider margins for notes

Performance features such as character and props lists, sound and lighting cues, and more

+ CHOOSE A SIZE AND STYLE TO SUIT YOU

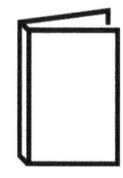  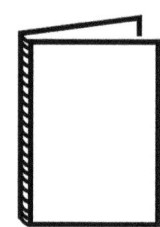

STANDARD EDITION
Our regular paperback book at our regular size

SPIRAL-BOUND EDITION
The same size as the Standard Edition, but with a sturdy, easy-to-fold, easy-to-hold spiral-bound spine

LARGE EDITION
A4 size and spiral bound, with larger text and a blank page for notes opposite every page of text – perfect for technical and directing use

| LEARN MORE | samuelfrench.co.uk/actingeditions

**Other plays by TERENCE RATTIGAN
published and licensed by Samuel French**

Adventure Story

Before Dawn

The Browning Version

Cause Célèbre

The Deep Blue Sea

French Without Tears

In Praise of Love

Man and Boy

Ross

Separate Tables

The Sleeping Prince

A Tale of Two Cities

Variation On A Theme

The Winslow Boy

**Other plays by TERENCE RATTIGAN
licensed by Samuel French**

A Bequest to the Nation

Less Than Kind (Love in Idleness)

Ross

While the Sun Shines

Who Is Sylvia?

FIND PERFECT PLAYS TO PERFORM AT
www.samuelfrench.co.uk/perform

ABOUT THE AUTHOR

(1911–1977)

Born in London on the 10th June 1911, Terence Rattigan was educated at Harrow (Scholar) from 1925 to 1930 and Trinity College, Oxford (History Scholarship) BA to 1933. He served as a flight Lieutenant in the Central Command, RAF from 1940 to 1945. In 1934 he had become a full-time playwright.

His many successful plays include *French Without Tears, After The Dance, Flare Path, Love in Idleness, While The Sun Shines, The Winslow Boy, The Browning Version, Harlequinade, Adventure Story, Who is Sylvia?, The Deep Blue Sea, The Sleeping Prince, Separate Tables, Variation on a Theme, Ross, Man and Boy, A Bequest to the Nation, In Praise to the Nation, Cause Célèbre*.

Terence Rattigan still holds the record of being the only playwright to have notched more than 1000 performances for two separate plays, namely, *French Without Tears* and *While The Sun Shines*.

During the war years, he had three plays running on Shaftesbury Avenue: *Flare Path* at the Apollo, *While The Sun Shines* at the Globe and *Love in Idleness* at the Lyric.

He wrote screenplays of *French Without Tears, The Way To The Stars, Journey Together, While The Sun Shines, The Winslow Boy, The Browning Version, The Prince and The Showgirl, Separate Tables, The Sound Barrier, The Man Who Loved Redheads, The Deep Blue Sea, The Final Test, The VIPs, The Yellow Rolls Royce, Goodbye Mr Chips, Conduct Unbecoming, A Bequest To The Nation* – and collaborated on *The Quiet Wedding, The Day Will Dawn, English Without Tears, Uncensored, Brighton Rock, Bond Street*. His television plays include: *Heart to Heart, Adventure Story, High Summer, After the Dance* was shown in the performance series on BBC 2 in 1993 and *The Deep Blue*

Sea was recorded for the same series. In 1958 he was awarded a CBE, and in 1971 he became Knight Bachelor. Sir Terence Rattigan died in 1977.

For further information on Terence Rattigan, visit www.terencerattigan.com.

To join the Terence Rattigan Society, visit www.theterencerattigansociety.co.uk.

HARLEQUINADE

Produced at the Phoenix Theatre, London, on 8th September 1948 with the following cast of characters:

ARTHUR GOSPORT	Eric Portman
EDNA SELBY	Mary Ellis
JOHNNY	Henry Bryce
DAME MAUD GOSPORT	Marie Löhr
JACK WAKEFIELD	Hector Ross
GEORGE CHUDLEIGH	Kenneth Edwards
1ST HALBERDIER	Peter Scott
2ND HALBERDIER	Basil Howes
MISS FISHLOCK	Noel Dyson
MURIEL PALMER	Thelma Ruby
TOM PALMER	Patrick Jordan
MR BURTON	Campbell Cotts
JOYCE LANGLAND	Henryetta Edwards
POLICEMAN	Manville Tarrant
FRED INGRAM	Anthony Oliver

The action passes on the stage of a theatre in a Midlands town between 6 and 7.30 of a Monday evening

SCENE—The stage of a theatre in a Midlands town.

The set represents an unmistakable, if rather severely functional, fifteenth-century Italian garden, with, at one side, the balcony of a house, from the window of which is shining a light. On the other side is a broad flight of steps leading up to an archway. But these are at present obscured by a traverse curtain which is drawn across the right half of the stage.

As the curtain rises music is playing. **ARTHUR GOSPORT** *enters along the path up left. He is dressed in doublet and tights.*

ARTHUR *(entering; over his shoulder)*

    He jests at scars that never felt a wound.

He comes below the balcony.

    But, soft! What light through yonder window breaks?
    It is the east, and Juliet is the sun!
    Arise, fair sun, and kill the envious moon,
    Who is already sick and pale with grief,
    That thou her maid art far more fair than she:
    Be not her maid, since she is envious;
    Her vestal livery is but sick and green,
    And none but fools do wear it; cast it off.

Juliet, in the person of **EDNA SELBY**, *appears on the balcony above.*

    It is my lady; O, it is my love!
    O, that she knew she were!

EDNA *emits a melodious sigh and gives a sad shake of the head.*

She speaks, yet she says nothing; and what of that?
Her eye discourses.

He crosses to right of the bench centre.

I will answer it.

He comes forward a step, then leaps back.

I am too bold, 'tis not to me she speaks:
Two of the fairest stars in all the heaven,
Having some business, do entreat her eyes
To twinkle in their spheres till they return.
What if her eyes were there, they in her head?
The brightness of her cheek would shame those stars,
As daylight doth a lamp; her eyes in heaven
Would through the airy region stream so bright
That birds would sing, and think it were not night.

EDNA *emits another melodious sigh, and rests her cheek thoughtfully upon her hand.*

See how she leans her cheek upon her hand!
O, that I were a glove upon that hand,
That I might touch that cheek!

EDNA Ah me!

ARTHUR She speaks:
O, speak again, bright angel! — for thou art
As glorious to this night, being o'er my head,
As is a winged messenger of heaven
Unto the white-upturned wondering eyes
Of mortals that fall back to gaze on him
When he bestrides the lazy-pacing clouds
And sails upon the bosom of the air.

EDNA
O Romeo, Romeo! Wherefore art thou Romeo?
Deny thy father and refuse thy name;
Or, if thou wilt not, be but sworn my love,
And I'll no longer be a Capulet.

ARTHUR *(aside)*

Shall I hear more, or shall I speak at this?

In the intense excitement of his passion he gives a boyish leap on to the bench centre.

EDNA*'s glance momentarily wavers from the upper regions of the theatre, on which her eyes have been sentimentally fixed, since the beginning of the scene.*

EDNA
'Tis but thy name that is my enemy;
Thou art thyself though, not a Montague.
What's Montague?
Darling, are you going to do that tonight?

ARTHUR What?

EDNA That little jump.

ARTHUR Well—yes—I thought I would. Why? Does it bother you?

EDNA No, darling. Just so long as I know, that's all.

ARTHUR Sorry, darling. That's quite all right. Let's go back. *(He gets off the bench and moves down right centre. He calls to the prompt corner)* Yes?

JOHNNY *(offstage left)* 'Tis but thy name—

EDNA *(sharply)* No. Before that. I want to give Mr Gosport the cue for his little jump.

JOHNNY *(offstage)* What little jump, Miss Selby?

EDNA The little jump he does on to that stool.

JOHNNY *enters down left.*

JOHNNY *(entering)* Mr Gosport doesn't do a little jump, Miss Selby. *(He stands down left)*

EDNA Yes, he does do a little jump. He's just done a little jump.

JOHNNY He's never done a little jump before.

EDNA I know he's never done a little jump before. But he's doing a little jump now. He's just put a little jump in.

ARTHUR Look—I don't think I'll do the little jump, after all.

EDNA Yes, you shall, my darling. You shall do the little jump. It looked very charming—very youthful. *(To* JOHNNY*)* When Mr Gosport says: "Shall I speak at this?" he does a little jump on to a stool. Now what's my line before that?

JOHNNY *(going off)* And I'll no longer be a Capulet.

JOHNNY *goes off down left.*

EDNA *(resuming her pose)* Or, if thou wilt not, be but sworn my love,

And I'll no longer be a Capulet.

ARTHUR Shall I hear more or shall I speak at this?

He does his leap again on to the bench centre, only this time it is, perhaps, not quite so boyish as before.

EDNA
'Tis but thy name that is my enemy;
Thou art thyself though, not a Montague.
What's Montague?

While speaking she has appeared to be struggling to keep her composure. She now loses the battle and laughs outright.

Sorry, darling.

ARTHUR Does it look awfully silly? I won't do it, then.

EDNA Oh no—you must do it. Come on. Let's try again.

ARTHUR No. I won't do it if it's as funny as all that. I only thought it might help the boyishness of the line, that's all. *(He gets off the bench and moves down right centre)*

EDNA And it does. It looks very boyish. *(To the prompt corner)* Doesn't it look boyish, Johnny?

JOHNNY *(offstage)* Very boyish, Miss Selby.

EDNA I was only laughing at your suddenly putting in a thing like that, after our having done this play so many hundreds of times together and never a little jump in fifteen years until now—just before a first night.

ARTHUR All right. All right. Let's forget the whole thing. I'll say the line standing as still as the Rock of Ages, and looking just about twice as old. Let's go on.

EDNA It's silly to say that, Arthur. If you feel you're too old for the part you'll only get a complex about it.

ARTHUR *(moving centre)* I am much too old for the part. I'm not seventeen.

EDNA Well, if it comes to that, darling, I'm not thirteen, but I shan't let that worry me tomorrow night. It's all up here— *(She taps her forehead)* it's not just a question of doing little jumps.

ARTHUR I am *not* doing any little jump. That's dead, once and for all. Now, for God's sake, let's go on.

EDNA Besides, it's silly to think you don't look young.

> **ARTHUR** *sits on the bench centre and pulls up his tights.*

> That wig is very, very becoming. *(She shields her eyes and looks over the footlights at the audience)* Auntie Maud! Are you in front, dear?

> **DAME MAUD GOSPORT** *appears through the curtain across the right half of the stage. She is an imposing old lady dressed as the Nurse.* **ARTHUR** *rises and moves down centre.*

DAME MAUD I've just come from in front, dear. What is it?

EDNA How did you think Arthur looked?

DAME MAUD *(moving right centre)* Far too old.

EDNA Oh. Too much light on him?

DAME MAUD *(crossing towards the balcony)* Far too much.

ARTHUR *(moving up to the bench centre and sitting)* What about Edna, Auntie Maud? How did she look?

DAME MAUD Far too old, too.

ARTHUR Too much light on her, too?

DAME MAUD Yes. Far too much. *(She moves under the balcony)*

EDNA I don't think Auntie Maud sees very well. Do you, Auntie Maud, dear? *(To* **ARTHUR**, *in an undertone)* She's getting shortsighted, you know, Arthur.

DAME MAUD *(turning and moving left centre; firmly)* Yes, I do. I see very well. I had my specs on, and I was right at the back, and you both looked far too old.

DAME MAUD *goes off under the balcony.*

ARTHUR *(calling)* Jack! Jack! Where's the stage manager?

JACK WAKEFIELD, *the stage manager, enters down left. He is a grave-faced young man in the late twenties, and carries a script.*

JACK Yes, Mr Gosport. *(He moves left centre)*

ARTHUR *(rising and moving right centre)* The lighting for this scene has gone mad. This isn't our plot. There's far too much light. What's gone wrong with it?

JACK I think the trouble is they've crept in numbers two and three too early. *(He calls up to the flies off left)* Will—check your plot, please. Number two and three spots should be down to a quarter instead of full.

VOICE *(from above)* O.K.

JACK And you've got your floats too high, too. You're burning Mr Gosport up.

EDNA What about me? I've got an enormous searchlight on me from somewhere out there.

JACK *(looking)* That's the front of house, Miss Selby. It's in the plot.

EDNA Well, take it out.

ARTHUR No, you can't. You've got to have some light on this scene. We can't have it played as just our two voices coming out of pitch darkness, much as we both might like to.

EDNA Well, I don't see why you should skulk about in romantic moonlight while I'm on my balcony, being burnt to a cinder by Eddystone Lighthouse.

ARTHUR Let me see that plot.

JACK *crosses to* ARTHUR.

DAME MAUD *enters on the balcony.*

DAME MAUD As you've stopped, dear, I thought you wouldn't mind if I gave you one or two teeny little hints about this scene. It's the first time I've seen it from the front. You don't mind an old lady's interference, do you, dear? *(She sits on the downstage stool)*

EDNA *(rather too sweetly)* No, of course not, Auntie Maud. You know how delighted I always am to have your teeny hints.

JACK *and* ARTHUR *pay no attention to* DAME MAUD, *but continue to rearrange the lighting.*

JACK *(crossing to left centre)* Take it right down, Will... That's it. *(He sits on the stool left centre)*

DAME MAUD *(to* EDNA*)* Now when I played Juliet I used to rest my hand on my cheek, like this— *(She demonstrates)* using just the very tips of my fingers. Now as you do it you look just a little like Rodin's *Thinker*.

EDNA Oh. Do I?

ARTHUR That's too low. Now bring it up a bit.

JACK Bring it up, Will.

EDNA Well, you know, Auntie Maud, dear, tastes have changed a little since you played Juliet with Arthur's father.

DAME MAUD I know they have, dear, and more's the pity.

EDNA The theatre's gone through a revolution since nineteen-hundred.

DAME MAUD It was nineteen-fourteen I played Juliet, dear. I remember the date well, because the declaration of war damaged our business so terribly.

EDNA There's been another war since then, Auntie Maud, and I don't think you quite understand the immense change that has come over the theatre in the last few years. You see, dear—I know it's difficult for you to grasp, but the theatre of today has at last acquired a social conscience, and a social purpose.

JOHNNY enters down right with some telegrams. He crosses to ARTHUR, gives them to him and exits down right.

Why else do you think we're opening at this rat-hole of a theatre instead of the Opera House, Manchester?

DAME MAUD Oh, I didn't know it was social purpose that brought us here. I thought it was C.E.M.A.

EDNA C.E.M.A. is social purpose.

DAME MAUD Is it, dear? Fancy!

EDNA sits on the upstage stool.

ARTHUR *(coming down right centre; still lighting)* Take it down. That's too high.

JACK *(calling)* Too high, Will.

GEORGE CHUDLEIGH, an old actor, enters along the path from up left. He is dressed as a fifteenth-century Italian peasant, and carries a flute.

GEORGE *(coming below the balcony; loudly and with clear articulation)* Faith, we may put up our pipes and begone.

JACK *rises.*

ARTHUR What?

GEORGE Oh, am I wrong? I heard my cue, so I came on.

ARTHUR Well, kindly go off.

GEORGE Yes. *(He moves to go the way he came then turns and crosses to* **ARTHUR**) Still, you gave me my cue, you know. You can't say you didn't.

ARTHUR What is your cue?

GEORGE Well, it's really a pause, when everyone's stopped speaking.

ARTHUR My dear Mr—

GEORGE Chudleigh. George Chudleigh.

JACK crouches by the stool left centre, puts his script on it, and studies it.

ARTHUR My dear Mr Chudleigh, if every time there's a pause in the play you're going to come on to the stage and speak that line, it's going to make the plot rather difficult to follow.

GEORGE I meant that's just my cue to come on. My real cue is "high will".

JACK *(unruffled)* "Move them no more by crossing their high will."

ARTHUR moves down right.

He's quite right, Mr Gosport. *(To* **GEORGE**) That *is* your cue, but your line doesn't come till the next act and you ought to have been paying more attention. Now will you please get off the stage as we're rather busy.

GEORGE *(moving to right of* JACK*)* Well—that's all very well, but you said it, you know. I heard it quite distinctly. So of course I thought you'd cut a bit out and so I counted five and on I came.

EDNA *reads a newspaper.*

ARTHUR *(in a fury of impatience)* Get off the stage, you silly old man.

GEORGE *(crossing to left of* ARTHUR*; stolidly indignant)* Here. Don't you talk to me like that, young chap. I acted with your father.

ARTHUR I don't care if you acted with Garrick's father. Get off the stage!

GEORGE You'd better be careful, young feller, talking to people like that. It's not right.

ARTHUR Change that prompt perch to fifty-three, will you?

DAME MAUD *(rising)* You say you acted with my brother?

GEORGE *(crossing to the balcony)* That's right. In this play I was, too. I played Peter.

DAME MAUD Yes, I remember now. I remember you well. You were just as incompetent then as you are now.

GEORGE *(under his breath)* That's enough from you, you old bag!

DAME MAUD *(triumphantly)* What did you call me—an old bag? There you are! That shows exactly why you've never got on in the theatre. If you have a line like that to say, you don't mouth it and throw it away, you say it right out. It's a glorious word to say—bag. *(Enunciating)* Form the word with your lips, like that. Bag. *Bag!* Bag!

ARTHUR *(crossing to right of* GEORGE*)* All right, Auntie Maud. All right. *(To* GEORGE*)* Look, my dear chap, just go to the wings—there's a good fellow—and wait for your scene, which doesn't come for hours yet, while we get on with our work.

GEORGE I certainly won't. I've been insulted and I'm leaving.

ARTHUR *(crossing to right centre)* Nonsense. You can't leave.

GEORGE Oh yes, I can. I know my rights. What's more, I'm not just leaving, I'm retiring. I'm sixty-seven, and I'd have been fifty years on the stage, come April.

DAME MAUD My dear Mr—er—you really mustn't take on like this just because...

GEORGE *(brushing her aside)* I've never been a good actor, and when I look at some that are, I thank God for it. What's more, I've never liked the life — and I've never needed the money. Why I've gone on all these years mucking about with never more than a line or two to say, sharing dressing-rooms with chaps I detest is more than I can fathom. Well, I'm finished with it all now, anyway. Finished with it for good, and you don't know how happy that makes me feel. Good-bye, all.

GEORGE *goes up the path and off left.*

DAME MAUD *(after a pause; scornfully)* Can't even make an exit properly.

EDNA Must have a film job.

ARTHUR Oh, all right. One of the supers can do the pipes line. Break for an hour for tea, but don't strike this set. I want to rehearse the farewell scene before the show.

JACK *(moving centre; leaving his script on the stool)* Yes, Mr Gosport. *(Calling)* Break for tea, everyone! Back at six-thirty, please! Curtain up at seven-thirty.

ARTHUR Then I'll rehearse the duel.

JACK Yes, Mr Gosport.

ARTHUR And I could see those girls for *The Winter's Tale*.

JOHNNY *enters down right with some sandwiches. He crosses to* **ARTHUR**, *gives them to him, and exits down right.*

JACK Yes, Mr Gosport.

ARTHUR And then, if there's time, I can rehearse the jig.

JACK Yes, Mr Gosport.

DAME MAUD Oh, Jack—send someone out for some sandwiches for me—and a bottle of Guinness, would you?

JACK *(moving below the balcony)* Yes, Dame Maud.

DAME MAUD Better make it a couple of bottles. It's so good for my back.

JACK Yes, Dame Maud.

JACK *goes up the path and off left.*

DAME MAUD Good-bye, my children. I'm sure from what I've seen it's all going to be splendid.

DAME MAUD *goes off.*

ARTHUR Sandwich, dear?

EDNA *(to* **ARTHUR***)* No thank you, darling. *(She rises)* I'll have a proper tea for us in our room, my darling.

ARTHUR Thank you, darling.

EDNA Don't worry, my precious. That wig is a dream. And you can do your little jump if you want to.

ARTHUR *(moving to the bench centre)* No, thank you, darling. *(He sits)* Edna—I'm not too old for the part, am I?

EDNA No; of course not, my angel. Or, if you are, then I am.

ARTHUR But you're three years younger, aren't you?

EDNA What's three among so many?

EDNA *goes out.*

JOHNNY *enters through the curtain across the right half of the stage. He carries a throne which he places down right, facing left. He then goes off down right.*

ARTHUR Johnny, draw the tabs and rehearse some of the lighting cues during the break, will you? *(He rises)*

The curtain across the right half of the stage is drawn back. Two **HALBERDIERS**, *complete with spears, are revealed on the steps playing cards.*

(He comes down centre. Over the footlights) Miss Fishlock? Would you come to my room for a moment? I want you to take some notes on *The Winter's Tale*. *(He turns and sees the young men)* Would you come here, you two?

The two **HALBERDIERS** *obey with alacrity, and come down right of* **ARTHUR**. **1ST HALBERDIER** *is in the middle.*

(to **1ST HALBERDIER***)* Just say "Faith, we may put up our pipes and begone."

1ST HALBERDIER *(in a flat, faintly cockney accent)* Faith, we may put up our pipes and begone.

ARTHUR *(to* **2ND HALBERDIER***)* Now you.

2ND HALBERDIER *(going much too far, vocally and in gesture)* Faith, we may put up our pipes and begone.

ARTHUR *(pointing to* **1ST HALBERDIER***)* Right. You'll do it. *(He moves away to left centre and picks up the script on the stool)*

1ST HALBERDIER *(transported)* You mean—I'm going to have a line to say, Mr Gosport? *(He crosses to* **ARTHUR***)*

ARTHUR Yes. *(He hands him the script)* I'll rehearse you in a few minutes.

MISS FISHLOCK *enters down left and moves to* **ARTHUR**.

Ah, Miss Fishlock. Would you get in touch with the London office at once and inform Mr Wilmot that the six girls he sent up specially for *The Winter's Tale* are quite out of the question.

MISS FISHLOCK Yes, Mr Gosport.

ARTHUR *exits down left centre, followed by* **MISS FISHLOCK**. *The* **2ND HALBERDIER** *moves up the steps and collects the cards.*

1ST HALBERDIER Oh, Mr Gosport! *(To* **2ND HALBERDIER***)* Oh, bad luck, Cyril. *(He moves to the foot of the steps)*

2ND HALBERDIER I bet it was because you picked up his gloves at the station on Friday.

The **2ND HALBERDIER** *drifts off right along the steps. The* **1ST HALBERDIER** *looks round the stage cautiously, and finding himself alone, comes down right.*

1ST HALBERDIER *(in a hoarse whisper, across the footlights)* Mum! Mum! I've got a part. It's only a line, but it's awfully important... Yes, isn't it wonderful?

JACK *enters along the path up left.*

JACK *(coming down left of the* **1ST HALBERDIER***)* Who are you talking to?

1ST HALBERDIER *(confused)* Oh, Mr Wakefield. I didn't see you. It's only my mother. She's up there. *(He waves towards the upper circle)*

JACK Then I'm afraid you must ask her to go. You know the rule about strangers in front at rehearsal.

1ST HALBERDIER Oh, but can't she stay and hear me speak my line?

JACK No, I'm afraid not. She'll have to come back at seven-thirty, when we start.

1ST HALBERDIER But she has to get back to Birmingham tonight. She only came for the day.

JACK *(firmly)* I'm extremely sorry, but rules are rules, and Mr and Mrs Gosport are very strict about this particular one. She shouldn't be here at all. *(He moves to the bench centre and sits)*

FREDERICK INGRAM *enters under the balcony. He is dressed as Tybalt and carries a cup of tea and a sausage roll.*

INGRAM *(to* **JACK***)* What the hell does he want me for?

JACK The duel.

INGRAM Oh, my God. Not again!

The **1ST HALBERDIER** *has meanwhile been gesticulating across the footlights to his mother, making uncomplimentary and furtive gestures towards* **JACK***. When he has conveyed his meaning, he goes off down right.*

I'm slipping across to *The Feathers* for a quick one. Do you think I've got time?

JACK Yes, Mr Ingram. I'll warn you.

INGRAM *goes off under the balcony.*

JOHNNY *enters down left.*

JOHNNY 'Ere—there's a baby in a pram in the wings. Is that a prop in the play?

JACK Not unless they've considerably rewritten it. Is it alive?

JOHNNY Oh, I don't know. I'll just see.

JOHNNY *exits down left and re-enters almost immediately.*

Yes. It's alive. What shall I do with it?

JACK *(rising)* I suppose you'd better leave it there. Presumably it belongs to someone. My God! What with mums in front and babies in the wings it's not so much a dress rehearsal as old home week.

JOHNNY *exits down left.*

MURIEL, *a nondescript, rather shabbily dressed girl of about twenty, and* TOM, *a soldier, about ten years older, enter timidly through the arch up right. They stand at the top of the steps staring about.*

Yes? What do you want?

MURIEL *(in a strong Midland accent)* Could I speak to my dad, please?

JACK And who may your dad be? *(He moves right of the bench and slightly up stage of it)*

MURIEL He's an actor.

JACK Then I'm afraid you've come to the wrong theatre. Try *The Palace of Varieties* across the street.

MR BURTON, *the theatre manager, enters down left and crosses to* JACK.

BURTON Good evening, Mr Wakefield.

JACK Good evening, Mr Burton.

BURTON I hope you find our theatre to your satisfaction?

JACK How are your bookings?

BURTON *(sitting on the bench centre)* Not bad. Not half bad, considering what the show is. Of course, we've never had these two up here before, you know, but it's a big help that feller Fred Ingram being in that picture at the Super.

MURIEL *(to JACK)* Look—I'm sure it *is* this theatre.

JACK *(turning to MURIEL)* No, my dear. They've got a sort of circus here this week. The *Palace* is what you want. Through that door there, up the stairs and into the street. *(He turns to BURTON)*

MURIEL *and* TOM *go off slowly right, along the steps.*

BURTON Funny for them to choose to open up here, I must say.

JACK Social purpose, Mr Burton.

BURTON Social purpose? Now what the blazes is that when it's at home?

JACK As far as I can see it means playing Shakespeare to audiences who'd rather go to the films; while audiences who'd rather go to Shakespeare are driven to the films because they haven't got Shakespeare to go to. It's all got something to do with the new Britain and apparently it's an absolutely splendid idea.

ARTHUR enters along the path from up left and comes down left centre. BURTON rises.

Here's Mr Gosport. He can tell you all about it. *(To ARTHUR)* This is Mr Burton, sir. The theatre manager.

ARTHUR Oh, how do you do? My wife and I are simply thrilled to be opening in your beautiful theatre and this delightful town.

BURTON Thank you, Mr Gosport, and I can assure you it's a great honour for us all to have you both up here.

ARTHUR Thank you. As a matter of fact you've always been very kind to us here in Sheffield. *(He moves down left)*

BURTON But it's next week you're playing Sheffield, Mr Gosport.

ARTHUR Oh! What's this town, then?

BURTON Brackley.

ARTHUR Oh yes, of course. They added a week, didn't they? How idiotic of them!

BURTON That's all right, Mr Gosport. Great men are always a bit absent-minded.

ARTHUR *(moving in to left of BURTON)* Brackley. Of course it is. *(With a sudden change of expression)* Brackley! Good Lord! *(He crosses to left of JACK)*

JACK What's the matter?

ARTHUR I was just remembering something. Brackley! Good heavens! *(He crosses to the throne and sits)*

JACK *(crossing to left of* ARTHUR*)* Is anything wrong, Mr Gosport?

ARTHUR *is lost in a reverie.* BURTON *looks at* JACK *a trifle bewildered.* JACK *touches his forehead.* BURTON *nods.*

ARTHUR Tell me, Mr—er—hrrm, is there a square place in your town with a perfectly repulsive building in glazed brick with a ridiculous dome on top?

BURTON *(doubtfully)* The Civic Centre.

ARTHUR *(impatiently)* Yes, yes. And then, dead opposite, is there an enormous white concrete and glass object that looks just like a public lavatory?

BURTON *(too hurt even to protest)* The Civic Library, Mr Gosport.

JACK *(hastily)* Do you know this town, then, Mr Gosport?

ARTHUR Yes. Only too well. Only too well. I was here as a boy in repertory.

BURTON *(moving in slightly towards* ARTHUR*)* When exactly were you here, Mr Gosport? *(He gets out notebook and pencil)* Could you pin it to a definite date? I ought to ring up the *Argus* about this.

ARTHUR Well, let me see now. *(He ponders deeply)* Yes, I can tell you exactly. It was the year Gladys Cooper opened in *The Sign on the Door.*

BURTON I'm afraid I don't remember that, Mr Gosport. *(To* JACK*)* Do you?

JACK No. *(To* ARTHUR*)* I suppose you couldn't remember anything else that happened that year? A war, or something like that?

ARTHUR No, I don't think there was a war. There was some sort of commotion…

JACK A commotion? An earthquake?

ARTHUR No, no. Something to do with trains. They didn't run. And newspapers, too. There weren't any notices. And then I was made to drive a tram, for some reason...

JACK Nineteen twenty-six. The general strike.

ARTHUR Thank you. That's right. That's what it was called. The general strike.

BURTON *(writing down the date)* Nineteen twenty-six.

ARTHUR *(rising)* Excuse me... I must get a cup of tea before I look at six girls...

ARTHUR *crosses left and goes off under the balcony.*

BURTON Bit scatter-brained, isn't he?

JACK I doubt if you can scatter a void.

BURTON I thought he was supposed to be an intellectual sort of chap.

JACK He's an actor, Mr Burton.

BURTON Now perhaps you wouldn't mind giving me a bit more dope on the Gosports for the *Argus*.

JACK *(sitting on the steps)* All right, but very quickly. I've got a hundred things to do.

BURTON *(moving up to left of* JACK*)* How long have they been married?

JACK Fifteen years.

BURTON Any children?

JACK One—little Basil.

BURTON Oh. And how old is little Basil?

JACK Thirteen.

BURTON Up here?

JACK No. At school.

BURTON Going to be an actor too?

JACK Judging by his behaviour, yes. Besides—he's a Gosport.

BURTON I see. Now how would you describe these Gosports? Would we offend anyone if we called them the most famous married couple in the theatre?

JACK You wouldn't offend the Gosports, Mr Burton, which is the main thing. Besides, it's reasonably true.

BURTON Always act together, don't they?

JACK Yes.

BURTON Always as husband and wife?

JACK No. Usually as lover and mistress. The audience prefers that—it gives them such a cosy feeling to know they're really married after all.

BURTON Now, about this tour. How long is it?

JACK Sixteen weeks out, then London.

BURTON Oh. They *are* going to London, then?

JACK Only for four weeks. If you play in the West End for longer than that you become commercial.

BURTON I see. What after that?

JACK Belgrade, Bucharest, Warsaw, Riga and Moscow.

BURTON Oh. What about the Iron Curtain?

JACK The Gosports could make any curtain rise.

BURTON What plays are they taking?

> ARTHUR *enters along the path from up left. He looks at the pots on the wall and picks one up.*

JACK *Romeo, The Winter's Tale, Macbeth,* and a modern play in verse called *Follow the Leviathan to My Father's Grave.*

BURTON What's that about?

ARTHUR *wanders down left centre with the pot.*

JACK Here's Mr Gosport, he'll tell you.

BURTON What's the new play about, Mr Gosport?

ARTHUR Death. *(He puts the pot in the niche left)* My wife's got the best part in it. I only play the pencil- sharpener in the last act.

ARTHUR *goes off down left.*

BURTON Well, perhaps he'll tell more about it to the *Argus* critic.

JACK I doubt it.

ARTHUR *enters down left.*

ARTHUR There's a baby here, in the wings. It looks exactly like someone I know. Who is it?

JACK *(rising)* I've no idea, I'm afraid.

ARTHUR It's very careless of people, leaving babies in the wings. There might be a very nasty accident. Somebody might easily trip over it and ruin their exit. See that it's removed before rehearsal. *(He starts to exit down left)*

JACK Yes, Mr Gosport.

ARTHUR *(stopping)* And in future, if people bring babies to the theatre, see that they're kept in the proper place.

JACK Yes, Mr Gosport. Where's that?

ARTHUR I don't know.

ARTHUR *goes off down left.*

JACK Well, is there any more help I can give you, Mr Burton?

BURTON No, thanks. I think that's all. It only remains for me to wish you a very successful opening, which I'm sure you'll have.

JACK Thank you very much.

They shake hands.

MURIEL *and* TOM *appear suddenly on the balcony.*

MURIEL *(attacked with vertigo)* Oo—Tom! Look where we've got ourselves to!

JACK *(crossing to the balcony)* Madam—will you and your friend kindly leave this theatre?

MURIEL No, I won't. I've told you. I want to see my dad.

JACK And I've told you your dad isn't here.

MURIEL Oh yes, he is. He's not at the *Palace*, like you said. He's here. I've seen his name on the posters.

JACK Well, you can't see him now, anyway. Anyway, who is your dad?

MURIEL Gosport's the name.

JACK Gosport?

MURIEL Yes. Arthur Gosport. He's an actor.

JACK Oh. I see. *(He signs urgently to the prompt corner)* So you're the daughter of Arthur Gosport, are you?

MURIEL Yes, that's right. And this is my husband.

TOM How do?

JACK I'm most delighted to meet you both. I simply can't apologize enough for having been so very rude. *(To* JOHNNY*)* Oh, Johnny.

JOHNNY *enters down left.*

This lady is Mr Gosport's daughter, and this is her husband. Would you be so kind as to—er—look after them both? Just—er—show them around, would you? *(He makes a quick, violent gesture of his thumb, unseen by the two on the balcony)*

JOHNNY *(nodding)* O.K., Mr Wakefield.

    JOHNNY *exits down left.*

JACK Now, Miss Gosport…

MURIEL *(giggling)* Mrs Palmer.

JACK I do beg your pardon, Mrs Palmer. Now, if you and your husband would be so very kind as to step through that window there and down the steps, you'll find such a nice gentleman who's going to take such very good care of you both.

MURIEL Oh. Thanks—you're a pal. Come on, Tom.

    MURIEL *goes off.* **TOM** *waves cheerfully to* **JACK** *and follows her.*

BURTON Lor' love us! What will they think up next?

JACK Amazing, isn't it?

BURTON *(shaking his head, sadly)* It's a funny world ours, isn't it?

JACK Side-splitting.

    BURTON *exits down right.*

    JOHNNY *enters along the path from up left.*

    All right?

JOHNNY I'll lock 'em in one of the downstairs rooms. I'd better not shove 'em out as the doorman's off and they might get in again.

JACK Quite right. Which room will you put them in?

JOHNNY I'll put them in number three. There are six other girls there waiting for someone.

JACK *(wearily)* I wonder whose daughters they are. O.K., Johnny. Thanks.

JOHNNY *exits up left along the path.*

The **1ST HALBERDIER** *enters up right along the steps.*

HALBERDIER Mr Wakefield, do you think it ought to be—Faith, we may put up our *pipes* and begone—or *Faith,* we may put up our pipes and begone?

JACK *(moving up the steps to left of the* **1ST HALBERDIER***)* What about—Faith, we may put up our pipes and *(roaring)* Begone?

HALBERDIER That doesn't sound quite right to me.

JACK It sounds awfully right to me. What's happened to your mum?

JOYCE LANGLAND *enters along the path from up left. She is a good-looking, smartly-dressed girl. She carries a mackintosh. She comes down left and stands evidently a little awed by her surroundings.*

HALBERDIER Oh, she's gone.

JACK *(grimly)* That's very lucky for *her.*

The **1ST HALBERDIER** *wanders off right along the steps, still muttering.*

JOYCE Jack... *(She crosses to left of* **JACK***)*

JACK *(surprised)* Joyce! *(He kisses her warmly)* Why on earth didn't you let me know you were coming up?

JOYCE I didn't have time.

JACK What do you mean, you didn't have time?

JOYCE I've got some news for you which I had to tell you myself, so I just jumped on the first train.

JACK Oh, darling. How wonderful!

JOYCE *(disappointed)* You've guessed.

JACK Your father's changed his mind. Darling, you're a magician. How did you work it?

JOYCE You worked it. He was terribly impressed with your letter.

JACK So he should be.

JOYCE *(sitting on the steps)* Then I told him your war record.

JACK That was a mistake, wasn't it?

JOYCE You got the D.F.C.

JACK Only because the C.O. liked the pantomime I produced for the chaps. I say, darling, are we rich? *(He sits right of* JOYCE*)*

JOYCE We'll pay super-tax, anyway.

JACK Oh, darling, how marvellous! I don't have to work any more?

JOYCE Not in the theatre, anyway.

JACK Oh. But I do have to work?

JOYCE He's going to take you into the firm.

JACK Oh. I thought there was a catch.

JOYCE Darling, it's not a catch. Jack—it's not that you don't want to give up the theatre, is it?

JACK Good Lord, no! I'd give up the theatre tomorrow if I could.

The 1ST HALBERDIER *enters down left.*

JOYCE Well, now you can.

HALBERDIER Faith, we may put up *our* pipes and begone.

JACK *(rising and crossing to the* 1ST HALBERDIER*)* Look, old chap—do you mind awfully going and doing that somewhere else? I've got things on my mind.

HALBERDIER Sorry, Mr Wakefield. This is my great chance, you know—and I don't want to muck it up. *(Muttering)* That's it. I know. Faith, we may put up *our* pipes and begone.

The 1ST HALBERDIER *goes off down left.*

JACK *crosses to the steps, left of* JOYCE.

JACK Darling, I think I'd better finish the tour.

JOYCE *(rising; horrified)* The whole tour—forty-six weeks?

JACK No, no. Only England. After London they'll have to get someone else. But I can't let them down without fair warning.

JOYCE No. I see that. There's only one thing I'm frightened of though, Jack. Shall I tell you what it is?

JACK That I haven't the guts to leave them at all?

JOYCE *(moving down right)* It's not only the Gosports I'm worrying about. It's the theatre.

JACK The Gosports are the theatre. There is no theatre apart from the Gosports.

JOYCE Darling, don't exaggerate.

JACK I'm not. I mean the Gosports are eternal. They're the theatre at its worst and its best. They're true theatre, because they're entirely self-centred, entirely exhibitionist and entirely dotty, and because they make no compromise whatever with the outside world.

JOYCE Then what about this idea of theirs of theatre with a social purpose?

JACK Theatre with a social purpose, indeed! It's a contradiction in terms. Good citizenship and good theatre don't go together. They never have and they never will. All through the ages, from Burbage downwards, the theatre—the true theatre—has consisted of blind, anti-social, self-sufficient, certifiable Gosports. The point is that if I have the courage to leave the Gosports, I have the courage to leave the theatre. *(He moves to the bench centre)*

JOYCE And have you?

JACK *(sitting)* Yes. I hate the theatre. I shall leave the theatre without the faintest regret, and for a week afterwards I shall barely draw a sober breath in celebration.

JOYCE *(crossing to* JACK *and sitting right of him; with a sigh of relief)* And I'll be at your side in that. Good. Will you go and tell them now, then?

JACK Now?

JOYCE Yes. There's a break on, isn't there?

JACK *(slowly)* Yes. Is this a test of my courage?

JOYCE That's it.

JACK All right. I might as well get it over with. Besides, I'm giving them plenty of notice, aren't I?

JOYCE *(smiling)* Yes. Plenty.

JACK *(rising; annoyed)* I'm not in the least afraid of them, you know, if that's what you think.

> EDNA *enters through the arch up right at the top of the steps. She is in a dressing-gown and is chewing a sandwich.* JOYCE *rises.*

EDNA I'm a bit worried about the balcony, Jack. It seems very wobbly to me.

JACK It's being seen to, Miss Selby. Er—Miss Selby…

EDNA Yes?

> JACK *passes* JOYCE *forward to left of the steps.*

JACK Could I introduce Miss Langland?

EDNA Oh yes. How do you do? *(She comes half-way down the steps and shakes hands)* You're a serving wench, aren't you?

JACK Er—no. She's not in the company at all. As a matter of fact, Miss Selby—she's the girl I'm going to marry.

> JOYCE *turns to* JACK.

EDNA Marry! My dear, how wonderful! How simply wonderful! Oh, Jack, darling, I'm so glad. *(She embraces him warmly. To* JOYCE*)* And you too, my dear. *(She kisses her)* So pretty you are, and so young, and what an enchanting little frock!

JACK *moves down centre.*

Oh, I'm so happy for you both, I feel I want to cry and ruin my make-up. Arthur must be your best man, and I'll be godmother to your first. When's the wedding to be?

JACK *(exchanging glances with* JOYCE*)* After the provincial tour—when we come to London.

EDNA Oh, good! *(To* JOYCE*)* It would have been far too long a time to wait for him, wouldn't it—forty-six weeks?

JOYCE *(surprised)* Yes. I did feel that, I'm afraid.

EDNA Don't be afraid, dear. You're quite right to be impatient. I was, when I married Arthur. *(She strokes* JOYCE's *face)* Dear little child. *(She comes down right and sits on the throne)* I'm so happy for you. So you'll be coming to Europe with us, will you?

JOYCE *(coming down to left of* EDNA*)* Er—no, Miss Selby. I won't.

EDNA No? Well, perhaps you're wise. It's going to be rather uncomfortable for all of us, I expect. Still, won't you miss him, being gone all that time?

JACK Well—the fact is, Miss Selby—you see...

EDNA Yes?

JACK I—er—well—this is the point—I'm not sure that I'm going to Europe myself.

EDNA Not going to Europe? *(She looks mildly surprised, then appears to see daylight)* Oh, I know what you mean. Some nasty creature must have sneaked to you about what Arthur was saying the other day about Ronnie Williams coming to stage-manage for us. *(She rises and crosses to right of* JACK*)* But you mustn't worry, my darling. It was only because Ronnie Williams stage-managed for us for so long—practically before you were born, my darling—and Arthur heard he was out of a job, and you know how tactless he is, the poor old thing— *(She crosses to the balcony)* but he really didn't mean it, I know he didn't.

JACK *(desperately)* Look, Miss Selby—it's got nothing to do with Ronnie Williams.

EDNA *(turning)* You're hurt, my precious. I'm so sorry. *(She moves centre to* JACK*)* But I can promise you most faithfully that there was never, never any question of our not taking you to Europe. We all love and admire you far too much.

JACK Thank you very much, Miss Selby, but...

EDNA Now I don't want to hear anything more about it. Just forget the whole thing and pretend it never happened. You're coming to Europe with us. I promise you.

JOYCE Jack!

> EDNA *crosses to the balcony and turns.* JOYCE *moves in to right of* JACK.

EDNA Good-bye, you dear things. *(She blows them a fond kiss)* You look so pretty, the two of you, standing there together.

> EDNA *gives the nearest pillar a shake to see how firm it is and goes off under the balcony.*

JACK *(to* JOYCE*)* Look, darling, perhaps a dress rehearsal isn't the best moment to break it to them. What about tomorrow—or after the first night?

JOYCE *(crossing down right)* Or after Sheffield, or after London, or after the European tour? No, Jack, darling, something tells me that if you don't do it now, during this break, you never will.

JACK I could write them a letter.

> ARTHUR *enters down left. He looks at the pot in the niche.*

JOYCE I thought you said you weren't afraid of them?

ARTHUR *picks up the pot.*

JACK I know. I'll tell *him*. He's really much easier to deal with than she is.

JOYCE *(indicating* **ARTHUR***)* Well, now's your chance, then.

JACK *sees* **ARTHUR** *and starts violently. He braces himself and moves left centre.*

JACK Oh, Mr Gosport.

ARTHUR Yes.

JACK Could I introduce Miss Langland?

JOYCE *crosses behind* **JACK** *left of him.*

ARTHUR Oh. *(He moves away down left)* How do you do? Have you read *The Winter's Tale*?

JOYCE Er—no. I'm afraid I haven't.

ARTHUR Well, it's not a difficult part. It's a girl who's been abandoned by her father when she's a baby, and then many years later they meet...

JACK Er—Miss Langland isn't here about *Winter's Tale,* Mr Gosport. *(In a firm, measured voice)* She's my fiancée, we're getting married after the provincial tour, and I'm not coming with you to Europe.

ARTHUR Yes. I see, my dear fellow. Now what about those girls for *Winter's Tale*? Are they here?

JACK Yes, I think so. Did you hear what I said, Mr Gosport?

ARTHUR Yes, of course. I think I'd better see those girls straight away. Have them in, one by one, would you? *(He puts the pot on the stool left centre)*

JACK Yes, Mr Gosport. *(He calls)*

JOHNNY *(offstage)* Yes, Mr Wakefield?

JACK Are the girls here for *Winter's Tale*? *(He moves up centre behind the pillar)*

JOHNNY *enters at the top of the steps up right.*

JOHNNY Yes. Seven of them.

JACK That's right. Mr Gosport will see them now, separately.

JOHNNY O.K.

JOHNNY *exits up right.*

ARTHUR *(indicating the pot)* How do you like it here, Jack?

JACK *(crossing down left)* Much better.

ARTHUR *(to JOYCE)* What do you think, Miss—er—hrrhm?

JOYCE I think it's charming, there.

ARTHUR No. *(He picks up the pot)* I don't think I like it there very much. *(He puts it in the niche)*

JACK Mr Gosport, I don't think you quite grasped what I said just now.

ARTHUR *(annoyed at the implication)* Of course I did, my dear fellow. You said you thought the pot looked better there, but I don't agree.

JACK No. Before that. I told you I was getting married.

ARTHUR Getting married? I'm absolutely delighted, my dear chap. *(He shakes hands)* Who to?

EDNA *enters along the steps right.*

(he crosses right below the steps) Edna, I've thought of an entirely new way of dying.

EDNA Have you, darling? How exciting.

ARTHUR Bring on the tomb, someone.

JACK *(crossing up centre)* Yes, Mr Gosport. Johnny, give me a hand with the tomb.

JOHNNY *enters up centre.*

JOHNNY Yes, Mr Wakefield.

ARTHUR *(crossing to* JOYCE *and leading her down right)* Now, young lady—perhaps you would be kind enough to take up a position there—thank you. *(He sits her on the throne. To* EDNA*)* The beauty of it is in its simplicity. *(He brings* EDNA *to centre)* Now I must get you something to lie on. *(He takes her mackintosh from* JOYCE*)* Thank you. *(He crosses to* JACK*)*

JACK *and* JOHNNY *bring the tomb down centre.*

JACK Look, Mr Gosport, there's something I've got to tell you before you die.

ARTHUR *(moving with* JACK *to centre)* Well, if she can't do the quick change in time, she'll just have to wear the black velvet all through.

JACK But, Mr Gos—

ARTHUR That's all there is to it. I don't want to hear another word about it.

He twirls EDNA *round and spreads the mackintosh on the tomb.* EDNA *lies on it.* JACK *moves up centre, picks up a script from behind the pillar, crosses down right and sits against the proscenium arch.*

JOHNNY *exits up centre.*

Now. *(He stands below the tomb)*
Come, bitter conduct, come, unsavoury guide!
Thou desperate pilot, now at once run on,
The dashing rocks thy sea-sick weary bark!
Here's to my love! *(He drinks)* Oh true apothecary!
Thy drugs are quick.

He bends to kiss EDNA, *groans and straightens up.*
Thus with a kiss I die.

He falls leaning against the tomb with one arm outstretched in front of **EDNA**'s *face.*

EDNA *moves his arm.*

JOYCE *(rising; to* **JACK***)* That was wonderful!

ARTHUR *(overhearing)* Oh. Did you like it, Miss—hrrhm? I'm so glad. You didn't think it was too much?

JOYCE Oh no. Not a bit—I thought it was thrilling.

EDNA *(sitting up)* Jack, darling, don't you think your little friend must be feeling awfully cold, standing on this draughty stage in that little costume? Wouldn't she be much better off in a nice warm dressing-room?

JACK *(rising; resignedly)* Yes, Miss Selby. *(He leads* **JOYCE** *to the exit down right)* Darling, run along to my room, would you? It's number fourteen on the second floor. I'll join you when I can.

JOYCE All right. *(As she goes)* Now, don't let me down, Jack. Before the break is up.

EDNA Such a sweet little face.

JACK Before the break is up. I promise.

JOYCE goes offstage, followed by JACK.

EDNA Arthur, it's a lovely death, but I'm not absolutely sure it doesn't go on perhaps a hair too long. I don't think we'll put it in tonight.

ARTHUR *(rising and crossing down left, knowing he has lost)* All right, darling. I just thought it was worth trying—that was all.

The **1ST HALBERDIER** *enters right on the steps. He is still muttering.*

1ST HALBERDIER Oh, Mr Gosport. Are you ready for me yet? *(He comes down the steps)*

ARTHUR No. In a minute. I'm seeing some girls first. Just wait there. *(He indicates the corner down right)*

The **1ST HALBERDIER** *sits on the throne, still mouthing intermittently.*

All right, Jack. Ready for *The Winter's Tale*.

JACK *enters down right. He has a board with some papers clipped to it and a pencil.*

JACK *(crossing up centre and calling)* All right, Johnny. Send the first lady on, will you?

JOHNNY *(offstage)* O.K.

JACK *(calling)* What is the lady's name, please?

There are whispers offstage.

JOHNNY *(offstage)* Muriel Palmer.

JACK *(writing it down)* Muriel Palmer.

MURIEL PALMER *enters at the top of the steps right. She is followed at a few yards' interval by* **TOM**. **JACK**, *busy with his notebook, does not immediately look up.*

MURIEL *(coming halfway down the steps; with a joyous cry, pointing at* **ARTHUR***)* There he is! That's my dad! Daddy, I'm your daughter, and you're my dad.

TOM *comes down the steps to* **MURIEL**.

ARTHUR Er—what text are you using, Miss, er— hrrm?

JACK *(interposing quickly)* Excuse me, Mr Gosport, but I know about this young lady. She's been annoying us all the evening. *(To* **MURIEL***)* How did you get out of that room?

MURIEL A young man came and unlocked us and told me and six other girls to come on the stage separately as Mr Gosport was waiting for us.

JACK Oh God! All right. Well, now, are you going to go quietly or shall I have to ring up for the police?

MURIEL Ring up the police? Go ahead. I don't mind. I haven't done anything wrong. I just want a few words with my dad, that's all. That's my dad, all right. I recognize him from mum's picture on the piano.

TOM Even in this country you can't arrest a girl for talking to her dad, you know.

MURIEL You can't scare me, young man.

JACK All right. *(Calling)* Johnny! Ring up the police station and ask them to send a man round. We're having trouble.

ARTHUR *(crossing to the left end of the tomb; to* **JACK***)* Do I understand that this lady claims that I'm her father?

MURIEL Your name is Gosport, isn't it?

ARTHUR Arthur Gosport. Yes.

MURIEL *(chattily)* Well, I'm your daughter, Muriel. You've never seen me, because I was born after you left mum. This is my husband, Tom—he's your son-in-law.

TOM How do?

MURIEL And I've brought someone else along that I thought you'd like to meet. Tom! *(She signs to him to go to the wings off left)*

TOM O.K., Mu.

TOM comes down the steps, crosses behind the central pillar and exits through the arch under the balcony.

ARTHUR Just a minute. *(To* **MURIEL***)* You mentioned just now a character called "mum". Could you be more explicit, please? Where does this "mum" person live?

MURIEL *(coming down the steps to right centre)* Same old place. Number twenty-one Upper Brecon Road.

ARTHUR Opposite a puce, rectangular building—with a notice board outside, saying: "Thy Days Are Numbered"?

MURIEL That's right. The Baptist Chapel.

ARTHUR And is mum's name—Florence?

MURIEL Flossie. That's right.

ARTHUR *(whimpering)* Flossie! *(He moves away left centre and sits on the stool. With a wail)* Oh, no, no. It can't be!

MURIEL Oh yes, it is, Dad.

EDNA Arthur! You can't mean—

ARTHUR Of course it's true. *(Pointing tragically)* You've only to look at her face to see it. The living image of her dreadful mother.

MURIEL Well, really! That's a nice way to talk, I must say.

JACK *(coming down right of the tomb; taking charge)* Look, Mr Gosport—as we've never seen the lady's dreadful mother, perhaps there's some other way we could test her story. *(To* **MURIEL***)* When were you born?

MURIEL January the fifteenth, nineteen twenty-seven.

JACK When did you last see Flossie?

ARTHUR *(rising)* Don't cross-examine me! I don't know. I can only tell you that I am absolutely convinced of the truth of this girl's statement. This is my daughter, Mabel… *(He comes down stage)*

MURIEL Muriel. Mu for short.

ARTHUR My daughter, Muriel. Mu for short. *(To* **MURIEL***)* Why are you here? What do you want?

MURIEL Want? I don't want anything. Just to say hullo, that's all. It seemed silly you being in the same town, and for us not even to meet each other. Mum didn't want me to come, but I thought dad'll be interested to see what I look like, and to meet his son-in-law. Besides, I've got such a nice little surprise for you. *(Calling)* Come on, Tom.

TOM *enters under the balcony wheeling a pram.*

I want to introduce you to your grandson.

TOM *wheels the pram tenderly to the left end of the tomb.* ARTHUR, EDNA *and* JACK *are too frozen with horror to move.*

ARTHUR *(at length)* My—grandson?

MURIEL That's right, Dad. Come and look. *(She moves in to right of* JACK*)*

ARTHUR *moves to the pram and gazes down at its contents.*

ARTHUR *(after a pause; slowly)* It looks— *(With a sob)* like Beerbohm Tree.

EDNA *(hopelessly)* No, darling. The terrible thing is—it looks awfully like you.

MURIEL *moves behind the tomb.*

ARTHUR Don't say that, Edna!

MURIEL Yes, he's the image of his grandpa, isn't he? The ickle, chicka-widdy-biddy-woo. Go on, Grandpa, tickle his little tummy.

ARTHUR *(breaking down left)* I refuse to tickle his little tummy.

EDNA *(to* TOM*)* How old is it?

TOM Five months. You're Edna Selby; aren't you?

EDNA Yes.

TOM I saw you in Shakespeare once, in Birmingham. You were the Queen, weren't you, when Mr Gosport was Hamlet?

EDNA I have played it—yes.

TOM *(cheerfully)* Well then, in a sort of way, that makes you our little Ted's great-grand-mama, doesn't it?

EDNA No, it doesn't. Not in any sort of way, and please, please, don't say it does. *(Reproachfully)* Arthur—how could you!

ARTHUR *(pointing to the pram)* I am not responsible for Ted.

EDNA *(pointing to MURIEL)* But you are responsible for Mu.

ARTHUR *(crossing to right to the throne; tragically)* I was a mere boy—wild, hotheaded, irresponsible, passionate boy—a Romeo of seventeen...

EDNA And your Juliet was Flossie.

ARTHUR She was my landlady's daughter. I loved her, for a time, with all my heart and mind. She loved me too, in her way—but not enough. She never even came to the theatre to see me act. *(He leans on the back of the throne and speaks to the 1ST HALBERDIER)* Of course it had to end, as all such mad, youthful follies must. *(He moves above the throne to right centre)*

EDNA *(pointing to the pram)* It didn't have to end in this.

ARTHUR *(pointing at MURIEL and TOM)* "And I say unto you, the sins of the fathers shall be visited upon the children even unto the third and fourth generation." *(To the 1ST HALBERDIER)* You know the line.

EDNA It seems to have got up to the fourth generation far too quick. *(She rises and crosses to left of ARTHUR)* Oh, Arthur, it's not in my nature to reproach you for what is past and done, but I do think you've been terribly, terribly foolhardy. *(To TOM)* Please remove this.

TOM O.K. If that's the way you feel.

MURIEL *(to the baby)* Didn't they appreciate him, then? Come along, then. *(She begins to wheel the pram out)* Come along, then! Say ta-ta for now, Grand-daddy.

TOM and MURIEL wheel the pram off under the balcony.

ARTHUR *(in tragic despair)* Oh, my God! Edna! What am I to do?

EDNA *takes his hand in silent but loyal sympathy.*

Jack, what am I to do?

JACK *(crossing down left; reassuringly)* Well, Mr Gosport, they haven't bothered you at all for twenty years. I don't see any reason why they should in the future.

ARTHUR *(running to the top of the steps)* Yes—but that child! *(With a shudder)* That horrifying child!

EDNA *moves halfway up the steps.*

JACK *(crossing to left of the steps)* No-one need know about that. Ask your dau—Mrs Palmer, to keep the whole thing secret; and if I might venture to suggest it, send an occasional little present to them for the baby.

EDNA A nice little box of jujubes, flavoured with prussic acid.

ARTHUR I don't think it's in quite the best of taste to make a joke of that sort, Edna. After all, the creature is my grandson. *(In agony again)* Oh, God! My grandson!

EDNA *(moving up to left of* ARTHUR*)* Never mind, my darling. These things can happen to any of us.

ARTHUR But why, when I'm playing Romeo, of all parts? Why couldn't it have turned up when I was playing Lear?

EDNA That's life, my darling.

ARTHUR Of course, we shall have to cancel the performance now.

JACK Look, Mr Gosport—I really don't think you'll find it necessary to do that.

ARTHUR How can I play a boy of seventeen with a grandson in the wings, mocking me with that repulsive leer of his, every time I go on?

JACK Because it won't be in the wings. First thing tomorrow morning I shall go and see—er—Mrs Palmer's mother. I'd better have her address again.

ARTHUR Twenty-one Upper Brecon Road.

JACK *(writing it down)* Thank you. And what is her name?

EDNA Flossie.

JACK Yes, I know. I meant her surname.

ARTHUR Gosport, I suppose.

JACK Gosport?

EDNA What an odd coincidence!

JACK Mr Gosport—did you—did you marry Flossie?

ARTHUR Oh yes. She made rather a point of it, I remember.

EDNA Arthur! You mean your daughter isn't illegitimate?

ARTHUR Oh no. She's perfectly legitimate, I think.

EDNA *(annoyed)* Well, really! Of course, that puts an entirely different, complexion on the whole thing. It's going to make *me* look very silly—if that gets out.´

ARTHUR It all happened such a long time ago, darling, and I really didn't see why I should bother you with the whole, rather sordid, story.

JACK *(quietly)* Mr Gosport—when did you divorce your first wife?

ARTHUR Let me see, now. *(He comes down the steps to the back of the throne)* I left her to take a part in a revival of *The Passing of the Third Floor* back at Barnes.

JACK I said, when did you divorce her? This is rather important. You did divorce her, didn't you?

ARTHUR Yes, of course I did, my dear fellow, I remember perfectly.

JACK Did you divorce her or did she divorce you?

ARTHUR We divorced each other, my dear chap.

JACK In law that isn't quite possible, Mr Gosport. Who was awarded the decree nisi—you or your wife?

ARTHUR (*to* 1ST HALBERDIER) Decree nisi? What's that?

JACK It's the decision awarded by the judge in a divorce action.

ARTHUR A judge? I don't remember a judge. I'm sure if there'd been a judge, I'd have remembered. There was a solicitor—I know that—and a lot of documents to sign.

JACK (*his voice becoming gradually edged with horror as the truth becomes clearer*) Mr Gosport—one solicitor and a lot of documents don't make a divorce, you know.

EDNA *comes down to left of the throne.*

ARTHUR (*crossing down left*) My dear fellow, don't fuss! Everything was perfectly legal and in order, I assure you.

JACK You don't think it might just have been a deed of separation that you signed, and not a divorce at all?

ARTHUR Of course it was a divorce. It must have been a divorce. The solicitor's name was Jenkins. He had Commissioner of Oaths on his glass door, I remember.

MURIEL *and* TOM *wander on at the top of the steps.*

MURIEL Hullo, Dad. Just been having a look round the stage. Don't mind, do you?

JACK (*urgently*) Mrs Palmer, if I ask you a straight question will you please give me a straight answer?

MURIEL All right. Fire away.

JACK Is your mother divorced?

MURIEL Divorced? Mum? Of course not.

JACK (*quietly*) Thank you. That was what I had already gathered.

MURIEL Mind you, she's often thought of divorcing dad, but somehow never got round to doing it. *(She comes down the steps and crosses down centre to right of* **ARTHUR***)* Not that she's got a good word to say for him, mind you. She says he was the laziest, pottiest, most selfish chap she's ever come across in all her life. "He'll come to a sticky end," she used to say to me, when I was a little girl. "You mark my words, Mu," she used to say, "if your dad doesn't end his days in gaol my name's not Flossie Gosport."

JACK *(crossing to* **MURIEL***)* Your mother, Mrs Palmer, is plainly a remarkable prophetess. *(He leads her across right and halfway up the steps)* Would you and your husband mind returning to number twenty-one Upper Brecon Road as I have a rather important little matter to discuss with your dad, who will be getting in touch with you in due course.

MURIEL O.K. Well, ta-ta for now, Dad.

ARTHUR *(crossing to the foot of the steps)* Ta-ta, and I will arrange for three complimentary seats to be left in your name for the Thursday matinée.

TOM Thanks a million, Dad.

ARTHUR I'm not your dad, you know. *(He crosses to centre below the tomb)*

TOM In law, old cock, in law.

MURIEL *and* **TOM** *go off along the steps. There is a pause.*

EDNA *(crossing to centre, below the tomb; to* **ARTHUR***)* Darling, I must say it looks as if you've been very, very careless.

ARTHUR Darling, there must be some hideous mistake. The whole thing is absolutely ridiculous. Jack, you must fix it.

JACK *(coming down to the right end of the tomb)* Mr Gosport and Miss Selby—I'm afraid this is something that not even I can fix. You must face, both of you, a very unpleasant fact. You are bigamously married.

There is a pause.

ARTHUR *(calling)* Miss Fishlock!

EDNA sits on the tomb, right end.

MISS FISHLOCK *(offstage)* Yes, Mr Gosport.

ARTHUR Come here a moment, would you?

MISS FISHLOCK enters down left with notebook and pencil at the ready. She comes left centre.

Miss Fishlock, it appears that my wife and I have committed bigamy. You'd better ring up the London office at once and inform Mr Wilmot.

MISS FISHLOCK *(faintly)* Yes, Mr Gosport. What—did you say—you and your wife have committed?

ARTHUR Bigamy.

MISS FISHLOCK sways slightly. Then, clutching her pencil firmly, she bravely writes down the fatal word—or its shorthand equivalent.

MISS FISHLOCK Yes, Mr Gosport.

EDNA Silly word, isn't it? It sounds almost as if Arthur and I had committed a serious crime.

JACK I hate to alarm you, Miss Selby, but that is exactly what Mr Gosport has committed.

ARTHUR *(sitting on the tomb, left of EDNA)* You mean I might have to pay a fine—or something like that?

JACK *(gently)* Miss Fishlock, do you happen to know the maximum penalty for bigamy?

MISS FISHLOCK nods, biting her quivering lower lip.

ARTHUR What is it, Miss Fishlock?

MISS FISHLOCK *(in a whisper)* Imprisonment—for life.

There is a stunned silence.

EDNA And—does that apply to me too, Miss Fishlock?

MISS FISHLOCK No, Miss Selby. You haven't committed any crime— *(Nearly in tears)* only Mr Gosport.

EDNA *(aghast)* You mean they would *separate* us?

JACK I'm afraid they would, Miss Selby.

EDNA Oh, no, they wouldn't. They couldn't. If Arthur has to go to prison, I shall go too.

JACK I doubt if that is allowed, Miss Selby. Is it, Miss Fishlock?

MISS FISHLOCK No, Mr Wakefield. I don't know of any—prison—where—convicts—are allowed to take their wives with them.

The thought is too much for MISS FISHLOCK. *She bursts frankly into tears and runs off left into the wings.*

ARTHUR *(rising and moving down left; calling)* Miss Fishlock! Miss Fishlock! What an idiotic woman, to get so hysterical!

EDNA Oh, my darling, I won't let them take you from me. I won't! I won't!

ARTHUR *(moving above the tomb)* Darling, there's nothing at all to get so worked up about. I'll make a public apology, divorce Flossie properly, and marry you again.

EDNA But that would be such horrible publicity.

ARTHUR *(moving down left)* The Arts Council will fix that. *(Suddenly galvanized into life)* Now don't let's waste any more time. We've got to get to work.

His eye lights on the 1ST HALBERDIER *who, all this time, has been patiently sitting and waiting to be called for rehearsal.*

You! I'll do your line now. *(To* EDNA*)* Darling, do you mind taking up your position in the potion scene, after you've drunk the potion?

> EDNA *lies down on the tomb. The* HALBERDIER *rises.*

JACK *(crossing to right)* My God! How much did you hear of all that?

HALBERDIER Oh, that's all right, Mr Wakefield, I'm not a tattle-tale. Wish me luck, Mr Wakefield. This is my great chance. *(He crosses above the tomb)*

> JACK *moves down right and sits against the proscenium arch.*

ARTHUR *(crossing behind the tomb and meeting the* 1ST HALBERDIER*)* All right, Mr—hrhm. We're ready for you. Now, I'll give you your cue.

HALBERDIER Thanks, Mr Gosport.

ARTHUR Leave a five-second pause, come on, look down at the bed and see what you take to be a dead body. Now I want to get from your expression that you realize that this girl, at whose wedding you have been hired to play, has taken her own life, presumably because she couldn't face her marriage with Paris, and that she has died for love of another. Your face should express understanding of the undying conflict between spiritual love and this gross, mundane world.

> *The* HALBERDIER's *usual expression does not change.*

Well, if you can't do it, just look sad. Then turn and say your line to your fellow musicians who we presume to be offstage, there. *(He points off left)* Understand?

HALBERDIER Yes, Mr Gosport.

ARTHUR All right. Go off. Jack, music.

> *The* HALBERDIER *runs up the steps and off.*

JACK *(calling)* Panatrope.

ARTHUR The heavens do lower upon us for some ill.
Move them no more by crossing their high will.

After the correct time interval, the **HALBERDIER** *enters down the steps, acting hard. He comes above the tomb, gazes down at* **EDNA**, *and contrives to look very sad, sighing deeply and shaking his head.* **GEORGE CHUDLEIGH** *enters halfway up the steps and crosses to right of the* **HALBERDIER**, *who slowly turns and faces* **GEORGE**.

HALBERDIER } *(together)* Faith may we put up our pipes and
GEORGE }   begone.

EDNA *sits up.*

ARTHUR What? Oh, Mr—hrrhm—you've come back. *(He moves slightly up stage)*

The **HALBERDIER** *wanders above the centre pillar.*

GEORGE I just felt I couldn't desert you both in the hour of your great affliction.

ARTHUR Our great affliction?

JACK Oh, my God! How did *you* hear! *(He rises)*

GEORGE I was in *The Feathers*, and a chap in the company came in and told us how Mr and Mrs Gosport were likely to get a life-sentence for bigamy.

JACK Oh, God! The news must be half over Brackley by now.

JACK *exits hurriedly down right.*

EDNA *gets off the tomb and crosses down right.*

EDNA *(calling after him)* Don't worry, Jack. The company, I know, will stand by us. *(She crosses back to* **GEORGE***)*

ARTHUR *gazes for a moment at the set, crosses left to the niche and picks up the urn.*

Mr Chudleigh, it was very naughty of you to leave us so suddenly, but I think I know what was the matter—we all of us suffer from an occasional *crise de nerfs*.

GEORGE Crise de what?

EDNA Nerves, Mr Chudleigh, nerves. Now come with me and I'll give you a nice strong cup of tea.

GEORGE and EDNA go off together down right.

ARTHUR, during this, has been staring chin in hand, fixed at the set. The 1ST HALBERDIER has been staring fixedly, and despairingly, at him.

HALBERDIER *(moving to right of ARTHUR)* Mr Gosport?

ARTHUR Yes?

HALBERDIER You couldn't—let me have another line to say—sometime—could you?

ARTHUR *(abstractedly)* I'll keep you in mind

ARTHUR hands the urn to the 1ST HALBERDIER and exits down right.

HALBERDIER *(sadly)* Thanks, Mr Gosport.

JACK enters down the path.

JACK Too late! It's out of *The Feathers* and into *The Green Horse*, now. They've all heard it. *(He wearily subsides on the stool left centre)*

HALBERDIER *(approaching JACK timidly)* Mr Wakefield?

JACK Yes?

HALBERDIER Do you think I should give up the theatre?

JACK Why ask me?

HALBERDIER You know so much about Life.

JACK What has Life got to do with the theatre?

HALBERDIER It's an awful shame about that line. It came at such an important time, with Miss Selby and Dame Maud on, and after a pause and with a chance for face-acting. The London critics might have noticed me.

JACK *(sympathetically)* I rather doubt that. The potion scene comes very soon after the interval.

HALBERDIER Well, cheeri-bye.

The **1ST HALBERDIER** *hands the urn to* **JACK** *and exits down left.*

JACK Cheeri-bye.

JOHNNY *enters on the balcony.*

JOHNNY Mr Wakefield!

JACK Yes, Johnny? *(He puts the urn on the ground left of the stool)*

JOHNNY The lady in your dressing-room says I'm to tell you time is getting on and you're not to forget your promise.

JACK All right. Thank you.

JOHNNY *exits.*

DAME MAUD *enters down right.*

DAME MAUD *(crossing to centre, below the tomb)* What is this terrible news?

JACK *(rising and crossing to left of* **DAME MAUD**) Oh, Dame Maud, have you been to *The Three Feathers*?

DAME MAUD I just looked in for a little refreshment and heard this abominable slander. Jack, have some pity on an old lady and tell me it isn't true.

JACK I'm afraid it is true, Dame Maud.

DAME MAUD I see. *(She sits on the tomb)* Well, of course, I suppose you know who's at the bottom of it all, don't you?

JACK No, who?

DAME MAUD The Old Vic.

JACK Oh, I don't think so, Dame Maud.

DAME MAUD My dear Jack, are you quite blind? It's as clear as daylight to me. They stick at nothing, that lot, absolutely nothing. *(She rises and crosses to the balcony)* I'm going to ring them up this moment and tell them exactly what I think of them.

JACK No, Dame Maud, you mustn't. You really mustn't.

DAME MAUD And Sadler's Wells.

DAME MAUD goes off under the balcony. JACK follows after her hurriedly and exits.

The stage is empty a moment, and then a uniformed POLICEMAN walks on down the path with firm measured tread to left centre. He looks round him.

JOHNNY enters on the balcony with a rope ladder. He drops it over the front and fixes the upper end.

POLICEMAN Who's in charge here, please?

JOHNNY Mr Wakefield. He'll be back in a minute.

JOHNNY goes off.

JACK enters down left. He crosses to the POLICEMAN and stops dead.

JACK *(murmuring)* Oh, God!

POLICEMAN You Mr Wakefield?

JACK That's right, yes. Yes, I'm Mr Wakefield, Officer. Yes, that's quite correct.

POLICEMAN I understand you want assistance.

JACK Assistance?

POLICEMAN One of your chaps rang up to say you were having bother at the theatre.

JACK *(infinitely relieved)* Oh, that! Oh yes. Of course, I'd forgotten. *(He laughs, rather hysterically)* Well, well, well! Just fancy your taking all that trouble to come round here. I do think that's good of you, Officer—but as a matter of fact it was all a mistake—an utter misunderstanding...

POLICEMAN You're not having any bother?

JACK Oh no, no, no! No bother in the world. Not a trace of bother. Everything's quite perfect.

POLICEMAN Then I don't know what you're doing wasting our time...

JACK Oh, my dear old chap—I can't tell you how sorry I am about that. It's awful to think of you walking all that way from the police station on a wild goose chase. *(He works the POLICEMAN over centre and sits him on the tomb)* Look, sit down, my dear fellow, do. Make yourself comfortable and I'll get you a nice drink. A nice large drink. What would you like? Whisky?

POLICEMAN Aye.

JACK Yes. I thought you would. Just sit there and relax and I'll dash and get you an enormous zonk of whisky—

JACK goes off down right.

The **POLICEMAN**, *sitting patiently on the tomb, is evidently rather surprised at the extreme affability of his reception. He takes off his helmet and puts it beside him.*

There is a pause, then **DAME MAUD** *enters under the balcony. She does not at first see the* **POLICEMAN**. *When she does she utters one single hoarse and strangled scream, and sinks slowly to the floor at left centre in a dead faint. The* **POLICEMAN** *rises, startled.*

JACK *enters down right with a glass of whisky.*

POLICEMAN Here, quick! There's an old lady having a fit.

JACK *(crossing to* **DAME MAUD**) What? Oh, it's Dame Maud. Oh, Lord! I suppose she saw you—I mean—she goes off at the slightest thing, you know. *(Calling)* Johnny! Johnny! Come here quick!

JOHNNY *enters under the balcony.*

Give me a hand with Dame Maud.

JOHNNY Took queer, is she?

JACK Just one of her dizzy spells.

POLICEMAN I'd better lend a hand—I know my first aid.

JACK Oh no. Please don't bother. You really mustn't trouble yourself, Officer. It's nothing at all. She's always doing this. She's over a hundred, you know—poor old thing. Just sit down and be comfortable, and pay no attention at all.

JOHNNY *and* **JACK** *lift* **DAME MAUD,** *and move up left.*

DAME MAUD *(as she is carried off)* Get me a drink, for God's sake!

JACK *and* **JOHNNY** *carry her off under the balcony. The* **POLICEMAN** *sits on the tomb.*

EDNA *enters on the steps up right.*

EDNA Jack—are we doing the farewell… *(She sees the* **POLICEMAN** *and stands quite motionless, looking at him. She comes down the steps very slowly and walks towards him to right of the tomb. Sadly, resignedly and melodiously)* Ah, well. There is no purpose to be served, I suppose, in kicking against the pricks.

POLICEMAN *(rising)* Beg pardon, ma'am?

EDNA Constable—I only want to say one thing. In fifteen years my husband and I have never spent a single night apart.

POLICEMAN *(sitting; politely)* Is that so, ma'am? Just fancy!

EDNA Not one. If we are separated, I think we would die.

POLICEMAN Would you indeed, ma'am?

EDNA I want you to know that nothing can keep us apart. Nothing: and no-one—not even you, Constable—can come between us now. If you take him, you must take me too.

POLICEMAN *(after a pause; stunned with bewilderment)* I see, ma'am. I'll bear that in mind. *(He rises)*

JACK *enters down left. He carries a drink. He gasps as he sees* EDNA *with the* POLICEMAN.

JACK Oh, Miss Selby, Dame Maud has been taken a bit faint. She's calling for you urgently.

EDNA *(tragically)* What can that matter now? I've been telling the constable...

JACK *(hastily)* Isn't it nice of the constable to come dashing round just because he heard we were having a little trouble in the theatre—especially when we're not having any trouble at all—are we?

EDNA *(understanding slowly)* Oh. Oh, I see. Constable, dear Constable, perhaps you'd better forget what I said just now.

POLICEMAN I'll try to, ma'am, I'm sure.

EDNA Just a little secret between the two of us, eh? *(To* JACK*)* What a beautiful line of the neck the constable has, hasn't he, Jack?

JACK Beautiful.

EDNA *(crossing up left)* Good-bye, Constable, and thank you for your great, great kindness to us all. I shall never forget it.

EDNA *goes off under the balcony.*

POLICEMAN That was Edna Selby, wasn't it?

JACK Yes, Officer. You mustn't, you know, pay too much attention to anything she might have said to you. She's suffering from the most terrible first-night nerves.

POLICEMAN Oh, is that the way it takes them?

JACK *(crossing down right)* Nearly always. Now, if you've quite finished your drink, I'd better escort you out.

POLICEMAN Thanks. I can find my own way out.

JACK Oh. Well, it's rather complicated, and I wouldn't like you to be bothered by any of the other actors.

POLICEMAN *(following* JACK*)* Are they all suffering from first-night nerves, then?

JACK Nearly all of them. Come along, Officer. I'll just clear a way for you.

JACK goes off down right. The POLICEMAN remembers his helmet and crosses back to the tomb.

ARTHUR enters down the path. He tests the ladder. The POLICEMAN puts on his helmet. ARTHUR sees him and crosses to centre below the tomb.

ARTHUR *(explosively)*Well, really, Inspector! This is too much! I do think you might have waited until after the performance.

POLICEMAN Well—Mr Gosport, sir, I've got my work to do—you see.

ARTHUR But, my dear Inspector, you mustn't listen to a word my wife says. I can assure you we're divorced. There's no doubt at all about it.

POLICEMAN Is that so, sir? I'd no idea.

ARTHUR And anyway, we haven't spoken a single word to each other since the general strike.

POLICEMAN That's too bad, sir. Your wife gave me to understand quite different.

ARTHUR Of course she would, my dear fellow. She's out for publicity, I suppose. *(He brings the POLICEMAN down centre)* But I'll tell you something else, my dear chap.

(Confidentially) I'm not at all sure that my child is really mine.

POLICEMAN Good gracious!

JACK *enters down right.*

JACK My God! Mr Gosport, Miss Selby's ready for the farewell. *(He crosses to right of the* **POLICEMAN***)* Officer, come this way, please! Please come this way! *(He drags the* **POLICEMAN** *away from* **ARTHUR**. *In a low voice)* You mustn't pay any attention to him, either. Least of all to him.

ARTHUR *goes off under the balcony.*

POLICEMAN First-night nerves, too?

JACK Far worse than that. He's completely and utterly off his rocker. It's terribly, terribly sad.

POLICEMAN Lor' love us! But he can still act?

JACK Yes, he can still act. That's all he can do. Come along, Officer, please.

The **POLICEMAN** *and* **JACK** *go off down right.* **ARTHUR** *enters on the balcony.*

ARTHUR Give me the lighting for farewell, please.

The light comes down to give a rosy dawn effect. The curtain across the right half of the stage is closed.

All right.

ARTHUR *goes off.*

A moment later he re-enters with **EDNA**.

Let me be ta'en, let me be put to death;
I am content, so thou wilt have it so.
How is't, my soul? Let's talk; it is not day.

EDNA It is, it is; hie hence, be gone, away!

> It is the lark that sings so out of tune
>
> Straining harsh discords and unpleasing sharps.
>
> O! Now be gone; more light and light it grows.

ARTHUR More light and light; more dark and dark our woes.

> MISS FISHLOCK *suddenly flies on down right, her countenance transported with joy.*

MISS FISHLOCK (*coming below the balcony; in great excitement*) Mr Gosport—Miss Selby—I know you'll forgive me for interrupting you. I have important news.

ARTHUR Yes, Miss Fishlock?

MISS FISHLOCK I got through to Mr Wilmot and gave him your message. He was most calm, most kind, most helpful and most reassuring. He is coming down to Brackley tomorrow morning by an early train, in person.

EDNA How very good of him!

MISS FISHLOCK What is more, he gave me a message to pass on to you both. He says you are on no account to worry yourselves about this matter. He says he happens to know there can be no danger whatever of—of—what we feared…

ARTHUR (*triumphantly*) I knew it!

MISS FISHLOCK He says it will probably be necessary for Miss Selby to sign a document saying that at the time she married you, Mr Gosport, she was aware you were already married. That, of course, would have the effect of making your second marriage null and void.

ARTHUR Oh. That's splendid!

MISS FISHLOCK There can therefore be no question of your having committed an offence in law. Oh, Mr Gosport, he was so wonderfully brave. He went on to say that there should be little difficulty in your getting a divorce from this—this other person. Then, afterwards, should you and Miss Selby still wish it, you could get married again. Only no publicity, of course. And that, of course, would settle the entire problem once and for all. *(She beams gladly at the balcony, conscious of a duty well performed)*

EDNA How brilliant he is, isn't he, Arthur? I really don't know why anybody ever works for another management.

ARTHUR Thank you, Miss Fishlock. You've done extremely well. I'm very grateful.

MISS FISHLOCK I knew you'd both be pleased. Oh, Mr Gosport—I'm so glad—I really am. I do congratulate you. And you too, Miss Selby.

MISS FISHLOCK *goes off under the balcony, again in tears, but this time of joy.*

EDNA
ARTHUR } *(murmuring)* Thank you, Miss Fishlock.

EDNA Arthur, don't you think you ought to say a few words to the company? I know they'll all be overjoyed at the news.

ARTHUR Oh. Very well. *(He calls)* Jack, assemble the company, would you?

JACK *enters down right and crosses to centre.*

JACK They're mostly in front already, Mr Gosport. *(He looks over the footlights)* Remain in your seats down there—everyone else on, please. *(He sits on the floor down centre)*

MISS FISHLOCK *enters under the balcony and stands down stage of it.*

JOHNNY *and the* **1ST HALBERDIER** *enter down left.* **JOHNNY** *sits on the stool at left centre.*

GEORGE *enters down the path.*

INGRAM *and the* **2ND HALBERDIER** *enter through the curtains and stand centre.*

ARTHUR Ladies and Gentlemen—with regard to this subject of bigamy—the danger point is past. I am sure you will be delighted to hear that Mr Wilmot has discovered a way by which my marriage to Miss Selby can be rendered entirely illegal.

There is a little flutter of hand clapping.

Thank you very much. Nor would it be right to let this occasion pass without extending on your behalf, on Miss Selby's and on mine, our most grateful thanks to Mr Wilmot, without whose co-operation and—ingenuity—and *savoir faire*—this very happy result would barely have been possible.

There is another outburst of applause, louder than the first. Mr Wilmot's spies, one feels, are everywhere.

Also to Miss Fishlock, who, as usual, has had to do most of the donkey-work, and has done it, as always, far better than anyone would ever expect.

There is one solitary clap for **MISS FISHLOCK**.

And lastly, Ladies and Gentlemen, to yourselves for the great loyalty you have shown in this moment of crisis to my wife, that is to say, Miss Selby, and myself. A thousand thanks. And one other thing. I'm not a difficult man in the theatre, as you know, but I would like to have it perfectly clear that I consider a very great deal of time has been wasted during this break for tea. Please see that it doesn't occur again. And now—back to work.

ARTHUR *goes offstage.*

EDNA Just a moment, everyone. I also have an announcement to make. I know you will all be overjoyed to hear that Miss Fishlock, with characteristic ingenuity, has at last successfully completed the National Insurance forms for the entire company.

The company melts away as they came; INGRAM *and the* 2ND HALBERDIER *through the curtains,* JOHNNY *and the* 1ST HALBERDIER *down left.* MISS FISHLOCK *under the balcony and* GEORGE *along the path.* JACK *remains sitting down centre.*

ARTHUR *enters down left and climbs the ladder.*

ARTHUR Bravo. *(To* EDNA*)* Let's just finish the climb down, my dear.

EDNA Yes.

Then, window, let day in, and let life out.

ARTHUR Farewell, farewell! One kiss, and I'll descend. *(He climbs down two rungs)*

EDNA Art thou gone so?
Oh, Arthur—I've just thought of something quite, quite dreadful.

ARTHUR What?

EDNA Little Basil.

ARTHUR Little Basil? *(He calls)* Miss Fishlock!

MISS FISHLOCK *enters down left and comes below the balcony.*

MISS FISHLOCK Yes, Mr Gosport?

ARTHUR Ring up Mr Wilmot immediately and inform him that he appears to have made little Basil into a little bastard.

MISS FISHLOCK Yes, Mr Gosport.

ARTHUR *(coming down the ladder)* What's more, there's far too much light on this scene—don't you agree, dear?

EDNA Yes, dear, I do. Especially on the balcony.

ARTHUR Jack! There's too much from here and too much from there. *(He waves his arms to left and right)* Now is everyone ready? *(He crosses right to the curtains)*

JACK You can't get the lights much lower than this, Mr Gosport, or they'll go out altogether.

ARTHUR *(going through the curtains)* Nonsense, my dear fellow.

> *The curtains open revealing* **ARTHUR** *and* **INGRAM** *on the steps with swords crossed.* **ARTHUR** *is above* **INGRAM**. *Left of them, also on the steps, are the* **1ST** *and* **2ND HALBERDIER**s, *each with a pike, and* **GEORGE**. *During the dialogue the* **2ND HALBERDIER** *knocks over* **GEORGE**; *then the* **1ST HALBERDIER** *knocks over the* **2ND HALBERDIER**.

Now is everybody ready? I just want to do the duel.

DAME MAUD *enters on the balcony.*

DAME MAUD As you've stopped, dear, I thought you wouldn't mind if I gave you another teeny little hint.

EDNA Not just now, Auntie Maud. Do you mind? Perhaps tomorrow.

DAME MAUD Tomorrow will be far too late.

EDNA *(paying no attention)* There's still too much on the balcony, Jack.

JACK *(shouting)* Bring it down more, Will. It'll never stand it, Miss Selby.

EDNA I'm sure it will—the lights will never let us down.

ARTHUR Now, Tybalt, take the villain back again.
That late thou gavest me; for Mercutio's soul
Is but a little way above our heads,
Staying for thine to keep him company;
Either thou, or I, or both, must go with him.

INGRAM Thou wretched boy, that didst consort him here
Shall with him hence.

ARTHUR This shall determine that.

> **INGRAM** *and* **ARTHUR** *fight. At this moment, the* **2ND HALBERDIER** *falls.* **ARTHUR** *stops.*

(to the 2ND HALBERDIER*)* Mr Warbeton, again please be careful, young man.
INGRAM *jabs* ARTHUR *with his sword.*
(to INGRAM*)* I'm supposed to win this fight, not you. Let's go back to the beginning.
INGRAM *and* ARTHUR *again take up positions for the fight.* GEORGE *and the* HALBERDIERS *argue.*

JOYCE *enters right, halfway up the steps. She crosses between* ARTHUR *and* INGRAM *and comes down centre to* JACK.

JOYCE *(above the din)* Jack! Jack! Time's up.

JACK What? Oh, clear the stage, will you, darling? We're extremely busy.

JOYCE No, I won't. Have you told them yet?

JACK Told them what? Oh, that. No, I haven't. Look, darling, I'm afraid you'll have to for me, that's all. I can't leave these two now. I realize that. How can I let them go behind the Iron Curtain without one sane man to look after them?

JOYCE Sane? You're not sane!

Two Monks enter at the top of the steps and stand either side of the archway. The Duke enters down right. He moves up the steps holding a scroll above his head. All those on the steps bow to him.

You're as mad as they are. This madhouse has infected you too.

JACK Madhouse? This isn't a madhouse. It's just an ordinary dress rehearsal, that's all. Now clear the stage, darling.

EDNA Jack, dear, there's still too much light on this balcony.

JOYCE *picks up her mackintosh from the tomb.*

JACK If you take the lights down more than this, Miss Selby, they'll fuse.

ARTHUR *(to the Duke)* Again, please. That's too quick.

EDNA Let them fuse.

JOYCE It's no good, Jack, I'm leaving you. You'll never get out of this. It's bedlam, and you're in it for life. Goodbye, Jack, good-bye.

JOYCE *exits up the path.*

JACK *(following to the up-stage end of the balcony)* Joyce!

DAME MAUD *(leaning over the balcony)* Now that girl has talent. Who is she? Arthur, who was that girl?

ARTHUR *(crossing down centre)* I don't know, Auntie Maud. Get her name, will you, Jack?

JACK *(coming down centre)* I've got her name, Mr Gosport. It's Joyce Langland. She was my fiancée.

ARTHUR Good. We'll try her for *Winter's Tale* tomorrow. *(He crosses to the steps and goes up them)* Now this duel is getting very sloppy. Let's go back.

Those on the steps take up their positions again.

EDNA There's still too much light, Jack.

JACK *(standing on the stool left centre)* Yes, Miss Selby. Take it down more, Will. And try those thunder and lightning cues two, three and four.

The lights suddenly go out.

My God! They've fused.

Summer lightning plays fitfully on the scene, accompanied by distant thunder.

ARTHUR *(calling)* House lights. House lights.

ARTHUR *comes down the steps and exits down right. The house lights go up.*

MR BURTON *enters hurriedly up left and comes down the path to centre.*

BURTON *(in a frantic voice)* Take those lights out! It's seven-thirty. There's an audience in front. Look! *(He points)*

A row of startled faces gaze at the now visible audience, and then they scatter in panic to the wings. The house lights go out. There is a moment's Blackout, disturbed by summer lightning and a roll of thunder. Then the stage lights come on again, revealing an empty stage.

ARTHUR *enters down right. He crosses slowly to the stool left centre, picks up the urn, places it on the stool and contemplates it. All the members of the cast put their heads round the various entrances and whisper frantically to* **ARTHUR**.

ALL Mr Gosport! Mr Gosport! The audience is in front.

They beckon **ARTHUR** *to the wings, but he is oblivious. The faces vanish.* **ARTHUR** *walks slowly round the urn, then, dissatisfied with its appearance, picks it up once* *more and walks slowly up the path, places it on the wall in its original position, and exits up left.*

The curtain falls.

FURNITURE AND PROPERTY PLOT

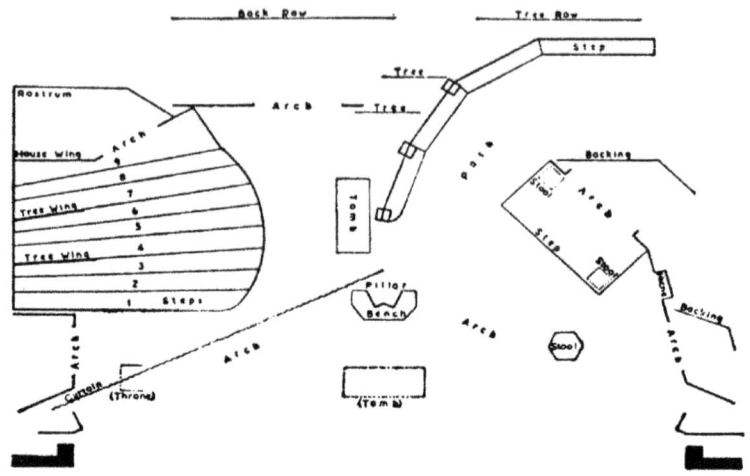

Onstage: On balcony: 2 stools, copy of the *Stage*
Stool, left centre
Stool centre by pillar
Tomb
2 urns, on wall

Offstage right: Throne, 2 swords, 2 pikes, pack of cards, telegrams, scroll, sandwiches

Offstage left: Script, stage manager's board, pencil, flute, cup, glass of whisky, perambulator, rope ladder, sandwiches, sausage roll, mackintosh

Personal: Burton: Notebook and pencil
Miss Fishlock: Notebook and pencil

LIGHTING PLOT

Set: Batten: 17 Steel Blue, 18 Middle Blue, 32 Medium Blue on Sky cloth
Floats: 9 Middle Salmon, 17 Steel Blue, 51 Gold Tint, 53 Pale Salmon
Ground Row: 9 Middle Salmon, 17 Steel Blue, 32 Medium Blue on Sky cloth
Spots to cover: Bench centre, 40 Light Blue; Stool left centre, 51 Gold Tint; Path, Balcony and area down stage of arches, 51 Gold Tint
Acting Areas to cover Steps right centre, 9 Middle Salmon
Pageant off right to cover Balcony, 40 Light Blue
Baby Spot off left through Balcony Arch, 54 Pale Rose
Perch (P.S.) to cover Bench centre, 40 Light Blue

To open: Batten: 32 Blue
Ground Row: 32 Blue, 17 Steel Blue
Floats: 17 Steel Blue on check
Spots: covering Bench centre, 40 Light Blue; covering Stool left centre, 51 Gold
Pageant: covering Balcony, 40 Light Blue

Cue 1 **Arthur:** "He jests at scars that never felt a wound." (Page 1)
Fade in Baby Spot through Balcony Arch

Cue 2 **Edna:** "Darling, are you going to do that tonight?" (Page 3)
Bring up Floats 17 Steel Blue, and P.S. Perch

Cue 3 **Jack:** "Take it right down, Will." (Page 7)
Snap down Floats to just in

Cue 4	**Jack:** "Bring it up, Will." *Snap up Floats as at Cue 2*	(Page 8)
Cue 4a	**Arthur:** "Change that prompt perch to fifty-three, will you?" *Change Perch to 53 Pale Salmon*	(Page 10)
Cue 5	Curtains open *Floats: 17 Steel Blue OUT; 9 Middle Salmon, 51 Gold, 53 Pale Salmon, IN on check* *Batten: 17 Steel Blue, 18 Middle Blue, 32 Medium Blue, FULL* *Ground Row: 9 Middle Salmon, FULL* *Acting Areas over Steps ON* *Spots covering Balcony, Path, and areas down stage of Arches ON* *Change Pageant covering Balcony to 53 Pale Salmon*	(Page 13)
Cue 6	**Arthur:** "Give me the lighting for farewell, please." *Floats: 9 Middle Salmon, 51 Gold, 53 Pale Salmon, just in* *Batten: 17 Steel Blue, on check; 18 Middle Blue, OUT* *Ground Row: 9 Middle Salmon, OUT* *Spots: all OUT* *Acting Areas: OUT*	(Page 54)
Cue 7	Curtains open *Floats: 9 Middle Salmon, 51 Gold, 53 Pale Salmon, on check* *Batten: 17 Steel Blue, 18 Middle Blue, FULL* *Spots: all FULL* *Acting Areas: FULL*	(Page 59)
Cue 8	**Dame Maud:** "…Arthur, who was that girl?" *Snap everything to ¾ check*	(Page 61)

Cue 9	**Jack:** "…She was my fiancée." *Snap everything to ½ check*	(Page 61)
Cue 10	**Edna:** "There's still too much light, Jack." *Snap everything to ¼ check*	(Page 62)
Cue 11	**Jack:** "…And try those thunder and lightning cues two, three and four." *Blackout. Lightning.*	(Page 62)
Cue 12	**Arthur:** "House lights. House lights." *House lights ON. Lightning stops*	(Page 62)
Cue 13	**Burton:** "…There's an audience in front." *House lights OUT. Lightning starts*	(Page 62)
Cue 14	After general exit *Snap on as at Cue 7. Lightning stops*	(Page 63)

VISIT THE SAMUEL FRENCH BOOKSHOP AT THE ROYAL COURT THEATRE

Browse plays and theatre books, get expert advice and enjoy a coffee

Samuel French Bookshop
Royal Court Theatre
Sloane Square
London
SW1W 8AS
020 7565 5024

Shop from thousands of titles on our website

 samuelfrench.co.uk

 samuelfrenchltd

 samuel french uk

www.ingramcontent.com/pod-product-compliance
Ingram Content Group UK Ltd.
Pitfield, Milton Keynes, MK11 3LW, UK
UKHW021845210426
5322IPUK00022B/483